First Facts

LEARN ABOUT ANIMAL BEHAVIOR

NOCTURNAL ANIMALS

BY KELLI L. HICKS

Consultant:
Bernd Heinrich, PhD
Department of Biology
University of Vermont, Burlington

CAPSTONE PRESS
a capstone imprint

First Facts is published by Capstone Press,
1710 Roe Crest Drive, North Mankato, Minnesota 56003.
www.capstonepub.com

Library of Congress Cataloging-in-Publication Data
Hicks, Kelli L.
Nocturnal animals / by Kelli Hicks.
  p. cm.—(First facts. Learn about animal behavior)
Includes bibliographical references and index.
Summary: "Discusses nocturnal animals and their behaviors"—Provided by publisher.
ISBN 978-1-4296-8268-8 (library binding)
ISBN 978-1-4296-9312-7 (paperback)
ISBN 978-1-62065-258-9 (ebook PDF)
 1. Nocturnal animals—Juvenile literature. I. Title.

QL755.5.H53 2013
591.5'18—dc23   2012002132

Editorial Credits
Christine Peterson, editor; Alison Thiele, designer; Svetlana Zhurkin, media researcher;
    Laura Manthe, production specialist

Photo Credits
Alamy: All Canada Photos, 6, Amanda Cotton, 21, Rolf Nussbaumer Photography, cover;
Dreamstime: Picstudio, 17, Seread, 13; iStockphotos: Kerstin Klaassen, 18; National Geographic
Stock: Annie Griffiths Belt, 10, Mark Thiessen, 16; Newscom: Danita Delimont Photography/
Rolf Nussbaumer, 9, ZUMA Press, 14; Shutterstock: Brandon Alms, cover (inset), back cover, 1,
Depiano (pattern), throughout, Dr. Morley Read, 5, Eliks (background), throughout, Mogens
Trolle, 19

Essential content terms are **bold** and are defined at the bottom of the spread where
they first appear.

Printed in the United States of America in North Mankato, Minnesota.
042012   006682CGF12

TABLE OF
CONTENTS

Active at Night 4

Safety in the Dark 7

Nighttime Hunters 8

Keeping Cool 11

Amazing Adaptations 12

Super Senses 15

Follow that Smell 16

Time to Rest 18

How Do We Know? 20

Amazing but True! 21

Glossary 22

Read More 23

Internet Sites 23

Index 24

Active at Night

At the end of the day, the sun sets. The night seems still and quiet. But outside there is a rush of activity. Mice scamper around looking for food. Bats and owls fly though the darkness. For these nocturnal animals, the day is just beginning. Nocturnal animals sleep during the day and are awake at night.

Animal Fact!

People are diurnal. They are active during the day and sleep at night.

leatherback
sea turtle

Safety in the Dark

Nighttime makes it easier for animals to hide from **predators**. A mother sea turtle comes out of the sea at night. She lays her eggs in the sandy beach. When the babies hatch, they crawl to the water at night to stay safe.

Animal Fact!

Some nocturnal animals will screech, stomp, or howl to scare away predators. These sounds warn others of danger.

predator: an animal that hunts other animals for food

Nighttime Hunters

Nocturnal predators hunt for food at night. Owls catch and eat mice, birds, and other small animals. Owls have rough feathers at the tips of their wings. This feature quiets the sound of the wings flapping. They can sneak up on **prey** without warning.

Animal Fact!

Not all nocturnal animals hunt. Porcupines eat flowers, leaves, and even chew on trees.

prey: an animal hunted by another animal for food

barn owl

black-tailed
jackrabbit

Keeping Cool

Nocturnal animals roam deserts during the cool cover of night. During the day, desert temperatures can climb to 100 degrees Fahrenheit (38 degrees Celsius). Animals keep cool by resting underground or in shady areas. At night, ringtails, jackrabbits, great horned owls, and other animals become active. They look for food on the cool desert.

Amazing Adaptations

Nocturnal animals have **adapted** to life in the dark. They have developed special abilities that help them at night. A snow leopard's eyes have cells that collect more light than human eyes do. These cells help the leopard see in the dark. Tarsiers' large eyes let in more light so they can see at night.

Animal Fact!

Tarsiers' eyes don't move. They turn their heads to see in different directions.

adapt: to change to fit into a new or different environment

snow leopard

13

Super Senses

   Some animals don't see well in the dark. They use other senses to find their way. Bats use their large ears and sharp sense of hearing to get around. They make **high-pitched** sounds that bounce off objects. Bats use these **echoes** to find food.

high-pitched: a sound that is high in tone
echo: the sound that returns after a traveling sound hits an object

Follow that Smell

The night air is still. Smells stay in the air for a long time. Nocturnal animals pick up scents to find food. Coyotes use their sharp sense of smell to track down a meal.

A snake uses its tongue to pick up scents. It sticks out its tongue and waves it in the air. The tongue sends a message to the snake's brain that food is nearby.

Time to Rest

What do nocturnal animals do all day? Some dig underground to sleep. Others rest in logs or nests. Red-eyed tree frogs hide under green leaves. They tuck in their legs and close their eyes to blend into the leaves.

Hippopotamuses stay in the water to keep their skin wet. At night they leave the water to munch grass in the cool night air.

How Do We Know?

It can be tricky to study nocturnal animals. Scientists use **infrared** light and cameras to record animals. As an animal moves through the light, the camera takes a picture. Scientists study the pictures to learn more about nocturnal animals.

Animal Fact! Scientists study animal droppings to find out what animals eat and how healthy they are.

infrared: rays like light that exist outside visible colors

The Humboldt squid, also known as the giant squid, is a jumbo-sized nocturnal animal. This giant predator can weigh up to 100 pounds (45 kilograms). During the day this squid lives in the safety of deep waters. At night it comes to the surface and hunts for food.

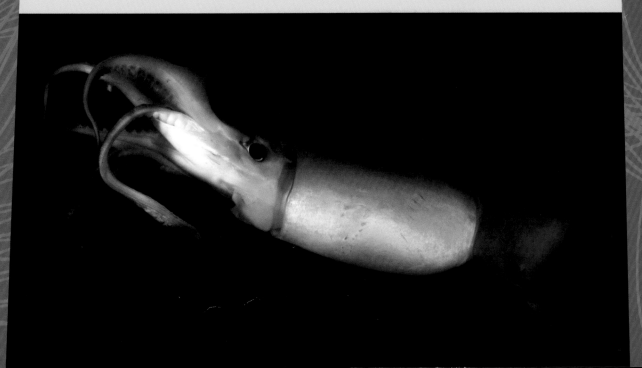

Glossary

adapt (uh-DAPT)—to change to fit into a new or different environment

cell (SEL)— the smallest unit of a living thing

diurnal (dye-UR-nuhl)—active during the day and resting at night

echo (EK-oh)—the sound that returns after a traveling sound hits an object

high-pitched (HYE-picht)—a sound that is high in tone

infrared (in-fruh-RED)—rays like light that exist outside visible colors

predator (PRED-uh-tur)—an animal that hunts other animals for food

prey (PRAY)—an animal hunted by another animal for food

scent (SENT)—the smell of something

Read More

Eck, Thomas Van. *Tarsiers in the Dark.* Creatures of the Night. New York: Gareth Stevens Pub., 2012.

Kalman, Bobbie. *Night Animals.* My World. New York: Crabtree Pub., 2011.

Stevens, Kathryn. *Night Creatures.* Reading Rocks! Mankato, Minn.: Child's World, 2008.

Internet Sites

FactHound offers a safe, fun way to find Internet sites related to this book. All of the sites on FactHound have been researched by our staff.

Here's all you do:

Visit *www.facthound.com*

Type in this code: 9781429682688

Super-cool stuff!

Check out projects, games and lots more at
www.capstonekids.com

Index

adaptations, 12

bats, 4, 15

coyotes, 16

deserts, 11
diurnal behavior, 4

echoes, 15

food, 4, 8, 11, 15, 19, 21

hippopotamuses, 19
Humbolt squid, 21
hunting, 8, 21

jackrabbits, 11

mice, 4, 8

owls, 4, 8, 11

porcupines, 8
predators, 7, 8
prey, 8

red-eyed tree frogs, 18
resting, 18–19
ringtails, 11

scientists, 20
sea turtles, 7
senses, 15, 16–17
snakes, 17
snow leopards, 12

tarsiers, 12